Crafting with Nature

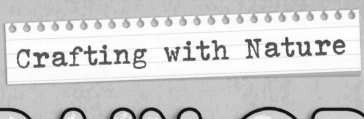

RAIN OR SHINE

Science and Craft Projects with Weather

By Ruth Owen

Enslow PUBLISHING

Published in 2024 by Enslow Publishing, LLC
2544 Clinton Street
Buffalo, NY 14224

Copyright © 2024 by The Rosen Publishing Group, Inc.

Portions of this work were originally authored by Ruth Owen and published as *Science and Craft Projects with Weather*. All new material this edition authored by Ruth Owen.

Produced for Rosen by Ruby Tuesday Books Ltd
Editor for Ruby Tuesday Books Ltd: Mark J. Sachner
Designer: Emma Randall

Manufactured in the United States of America

CPSIA compliance information: Batch #CSENS24: For further information contact
Enslow Publishing LLC, New York, New York at 1-800-398-2504.

Please visit our website, www.enslowpublishing.com. For a free color catalog of all our high-quality books,
call toll free 1-800-398-2504 or fax 1-877-980-4454.

Cataloging-in-Publication Data

Names: Owen, Ruth.
Title: Rain or shine: science and craft projects with weather / Ruth Owen.
Description: New York : Enslow Publishing, 2024. | Series: Crafting with nature | Includes glossary and index.
Identifiers: ISBN 9781978535664 (pbk.) | ISBN 9781978535671 (library bound) | ISBN 9781978535688 (ebook)
Subjects: LCSH: Weather--Juvenile literature. | Science--Juvenile literature. | Science projects--Juvenile literature.
Classification: LCC QC981.3 O94 2024 | DDC 551.5078--dc23

Photo Credits:
Cover, 1, 4–5, 6–7, 10–11, 12–13, 14–15, 16–17, 18–19, 22, 23 (top), 24, 25 (top right), 26–27 ©
Shutterstock; 8–9, 20–21, 25 (top left), 25 (bottom), 28–29 © Ruby Tuesday Books Ltd;
23 (bottom) © National Weather Service, Aberdeen, South Dakota.

Find us on

CONTENTS

WHAT'S THE WEATHER?

It's snowing! Phew, it's hot today! Does it look like rain? Wow, it's very windy. Can I hear the rumbling of thunder? **There are many different types of weather. They all affect the clothes we wear and the things we can do outside.**

Weather can be very different from place to place, even at the same time of year. In winter there may be lots of snow in Chicago. A winter day in Florida, however, may be so warm and sunny that people visit the beach.

This book is all about the weather. You will find out what makes different types of weather happen. You will also get the chance to make some fun weather crafts!

a snowy day

a windy day

Windy Weather

Wind is a type of weather that happens when air moves around. You can't see the wind, but when it blows your hair around your face or nearly pushes you over, you know it's there!

5

IS IT HOT OR COLD TODAY?

A big part of studying the weather is knowing about temperatures. The temperature is how hot or cold it is.

To measure the temperature, we use units of measurement called **degrees.** Instead of writing the word "degrees," we can use a **symbol** that looks like a tiny circle: °.

You can find out the temperature by looking at a thermometer. The red **liquid** inside the thermometer goes up as the temperature gets hotter and down as the temperature cools. The top of the red line shows how many degrees the temperature is against a scale.

On a sunny summer day, the hot temperature can melt ice cream!

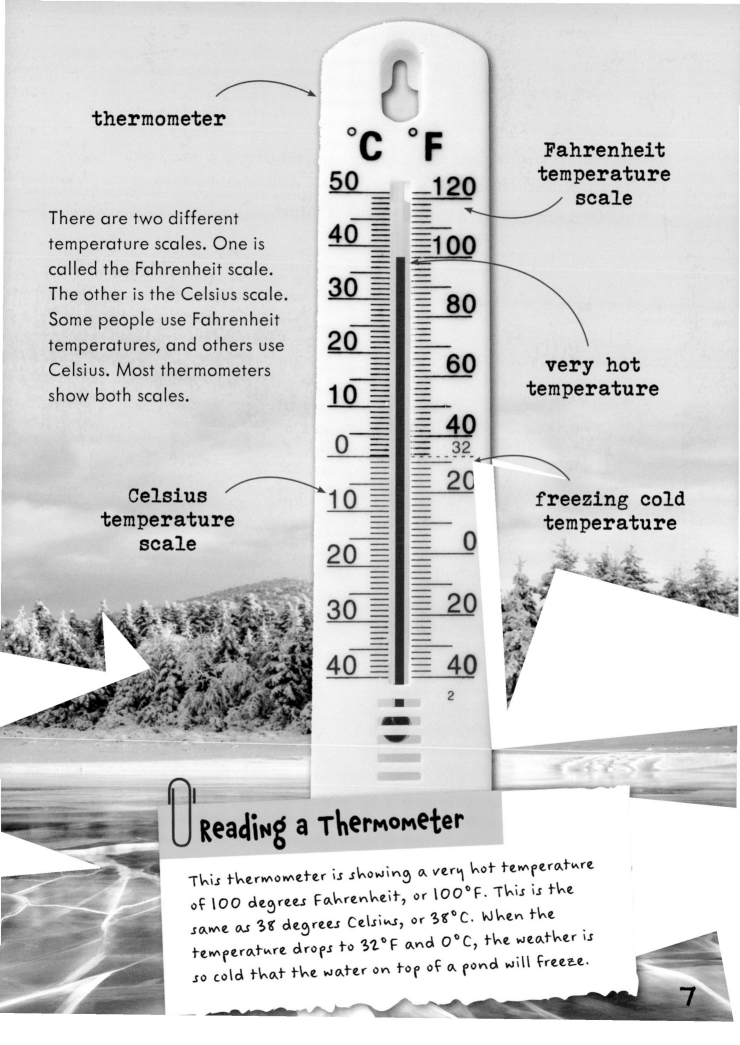

thermometer

Fahrenheit temperature scale

There are two different temperature scales. One is called the Fahrenheit scale. The other is the Celsius scale. Some people use Fahrenheit temperatures, and others use Celsius. Most thermometers show both scales.

very hot temperature

Celsius temperature scale

freezing cold temperature

°C   °F

Reading a Thermometer

This thermometer is showing a very hot temperature of 100 degrees Fahrenheit, or 100°F. This is the same as 38 degrees Celsius, or 38°C. When the temperature drops to 32°F and 0°C, the weather is so cold that the water on top of a pond will freeze.

WAX SUNCATCHER

This colorful handprint suncatcher can be hung in a window where it will catch the sun's rays. And on dull, cloudy days, it will bring some cheery color to your window.

You will need:

- Yellow, orange, and red finger paint
- 3 flat dishes or containers
- White construction paper
- Scissors
- A piece of cardboard at least 8 inches by 8 inches (20 x 20 cm)
- A ruler
- A paintbrush
- Glue
- Waxed paper
- Yellow, orange, and red wax crayons
- A cheese grater
- A small bowl
- An iron
- Cotton or ribbon
- An adult to be your teammate

GET CRAFTING:

1. Ask an adult to help you pour the paint into flat containers or dishes.

2. On the construction paper, make up to 10 paint handprints in yellow, orange, and red. Then ask an adult to help you cut out the handprints.

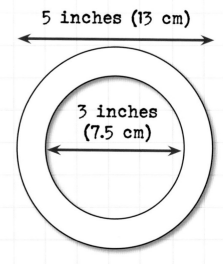

5 inches (13 cm)

3 inches (7.5 cm)

3. Ask an adult to cut a doughnut shape from the cardboard. It should measure about 5 inches (13 cm) across. The inner circle should measure about 3 inches (7.5 cm) across.

4 Paint the doughnut shape yellow. Glue the handprints to the back of the doughnut shape to make the sun.

5 Ask an adult to cut two circles of waxed paper that are 4 inches (10 cm) across.

6 Grate the crayons into a small bowl, being very careful not to rub your fingers against the grater. Mix up the different-colored pieces of crayon in the bowl.

7 Sprinkle some grated crayon onto one of the waxed-paper circles. Then place the other waxed-paper circle on top, so you have a crayon sandwich.

8 Now ask an adult to iron the waxed-paper crayon sandwich using a cool iron. Keep ironing until the crayons melt and swirl together.

9 Finally, glue the crayon sandwich to the back of your sun.

10 Hang your suncatcher in a sunny window. When light shines through the center of the sun, it will make colors in the room!

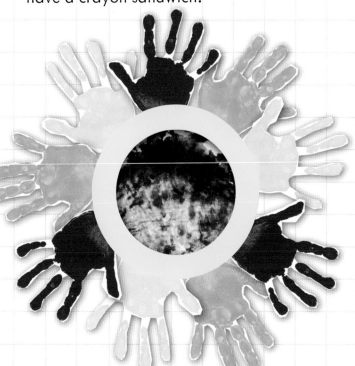

WATER ON THE MOVE

Clouds appear in the sky, and then suddenly it starts to rain. We know the rain is coming from clouds, but how did all that water get up into the sky? It's all because of the water cycle.

Warmth from the sun turns water from ponds, rivers, the ocean, and even puddles into a **gas** called **water vapor.**

The water vapor rises up high into the sky. Many miles (km) above Earth, the air is extremely cold. The cold air turns the vapor back into tiny drops of water.

This puddle is getting smaller as the water becomes vapor.

Water Vapor

Water on Earth is changing into water vapor all day, every day. It's not possible to see water vapor, but it is in the air all around us.

The waterdrops stick to bits of dust in the air. Billions of tiny waterdrops join together to make clouds.

Inside a cloud, the waterdrops get bigger and heavier, until finally they fall back to Earth as rain. The water cycle is complete.

Around and around, water on Earth is always moving through the water cycle.

clouds

A BEAD WATER CYCLE

This fun project is a perfect mix of weather science and crafting! Make bead friendship bracelets that will help you and your friends remember all the stages of the water cycle.

You will need:
- Yellow, clear, white, blue, and green beads
- Leather cord or elastic thread
- Scissors

GET CRAFTING:

1. You can buy beads from bead shops, craft stores, and online. You can also ask the adults you know if they have any strings of beads or jewelry they no longer want so that you can recycle the beads.

2. Here is what the different-colored beads will stand for in your bracelet.

yellow beads = the sun

clear beads = water vapor

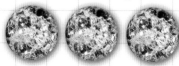

white beads = clouds

blue beads = rain

elastic thread

green beads = Earth

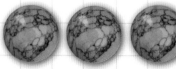

3 Start stringing the beads onto the cord or elastic. String the beads in this order:

First, add a yellow bead for the sun shining. Then add a clear bead for water turning to invisible vapor.

Next, string a white bead to show vapor turning back into water to form clouds.

Then add a blue bead for raindrops. Finish the pattern with a green bead to show the rain falling on Earth.

4 Now repeat the pattern again to show how water goes through the stages of the water cycle again and again.

5 You can create the water cycle pattern by stringing single-colored beads, or string together two beads for each stage of the water cycle. Have fun!

A raindrop might be as big as the fingernail on your little finger, or as small as a grain of sugar. No matter its size, a single raindrop that falls from a cloud can be made from millions of tiny waterdrops.

When raindrops hit your umbrella, they may have come from a cloud that's floating 3 miles (4.8 km) above your head!

Rain splashes into puddles, ponds, rivers, and the ocean.

Some rain falls on land, too, and soaks into the ground.

A raincoat, rubber boots, and umbrella are just right for a wet, rainy day.

raindrops on a leaf

Once the rainwater is back on Earth, it may go through the water cycle again within a few days or even hours. The water might stay on Earth for thousands of years, however.

A puddle is a good place for animals to take a bath!

When No Rain Falls

Sometimes no rain, or less rain than expected, falls in an area. After many months, or even years, the lack of rain causes a **drought**. Lakes and rivers dry up so people and animals do not have enough water to drink. **Crops** cannot grow without water, so people do not have enough to eat.

This crop is struggling to grow in dry ground caused by a drought.

IT'S RAINING COLLAGE

A collage is a picture made by sticking lots of materials onto a background. Get crafting and make your own collage all about rain.

You will need:
- A large sheet of construction paper
- A paintbrush
- Blue paint
- Scissors
- Glue stick
- Aluminum foil
- Cotton balls
- Colored paper, felt, and fabric scraps
- A hole punch
- Old magazines
- An adult to be your teammate and to help with cutting

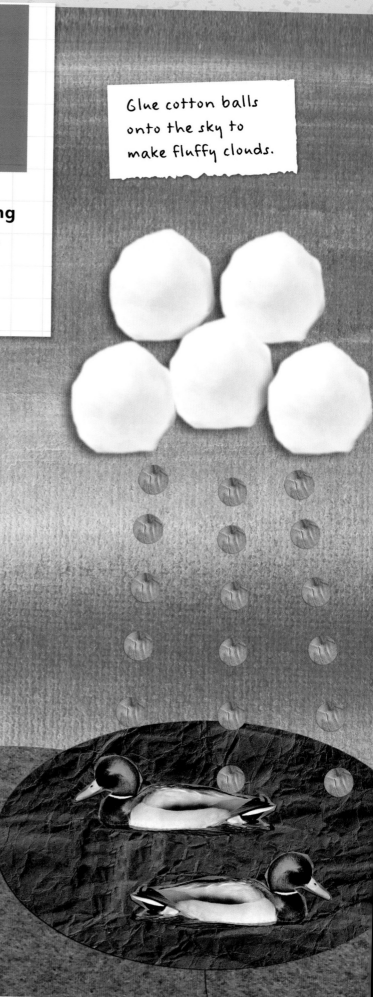

Glue cotton balls onto the sky to make fluffy clouds.

Make a pond using blue paper or fabric.

Cut photographs from old magazines.

GET CRAFTING:

1. Paint the sheet of paper blue to make the sky.

2. At the bottom of your picture, you can make hills using colored paper or fabric. Ask an adult to help you with any cutting.

3. Now it's time to make the rainy scene. You can make a picture like the one on this page, or get creative with your own ideas. Look at the labels on this collage picture for some ideas to get you started.

Use a hole punch to cut tiny circles of foil as raindrops.

Make puddles from foil.

17

Sometimes, the temperature is so cold that the tiny waterdrops in clouds freeze. Then they become pieces of ice called crystals.

A snowplow clears snow from a road during a blizzard.

The ice crystals stick together and form snowflakes. No two snowflakes look the same. Every snowflake has its own pattern.

When a cloud contains snowflakes, snow falls to the ground instead of rain.

Sometimes storms called **blizzards** happen. During a blizzard, huge amounts of snow fall, and there are very strong winds.

Snowflake Patterns

Every snowflake has six arms that branch out from its center. A snowflake is also symmetrical through its center. This means if you draw a line through the snowflake's middle, the two halves will mirror each other.

line of symmetry

close-up photo of a real snowflake

SYMMETRICAL SNOWFLAKES

This project shows you how to make paper snowflake decorations. Each snowflake can be a different design, but remember—their patterns must be symmetrical and they must each have six arms.

You will need:
- Sheets of white paper
- Scissors
- Tape or glue
- Ribbon or string for hanging the snowflakes

GET CRAFTING:

1. Ask an adult to help you cut the paper into strips about 5 inches (13 cm) long. Cut some strips that are 1 inch (2.5 cm) wide, and some that are 0.5 inch (1.3 cm) wide.

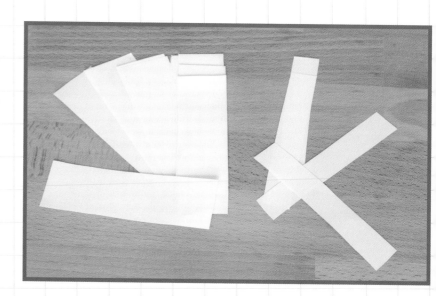

2. Roll the paper strips into circular coils and use the tape or glue to secure them. Make large coils and small coils, but remember, for your snowflake to be symmetrical you must have coils that match each other for size.

3 Now, try making snowflake shapes using the coils.
You can mix up large coils and small coils.

4 Once you have made a snowflake shape that you like, glue or tape all the coils together. Tie a piece of ribbon or string through one of the coils at the end of an arm. Your snowflake is ready to hang up.

5 Try making lots of different snowflakes and then hang them up together.

IT'S RAINING HAILSTONES

It's not only rain and snow that falls from clouds. Sometimes solid chunks of ice beat down on us from the sky—hailstones!

Hailstones form inside huge thunderstorm clouds, where it is very windy.

Inside the cloud, the wind blows waterdrops up high, where it is cold. The drops freeze into icy balls, or hailstones.

hailstones

The hailstones then fall back down in the cloud, and more waterdrops stick to them. Then they are blown up high again, and this new water freezes, too.

As more water sticks to each hailstone and then freezes, the hailstone gets bigger and bigger. Finally, the hailstones fall down to Earth!

It's possible to see the layers of water that froze inside this hailstone.

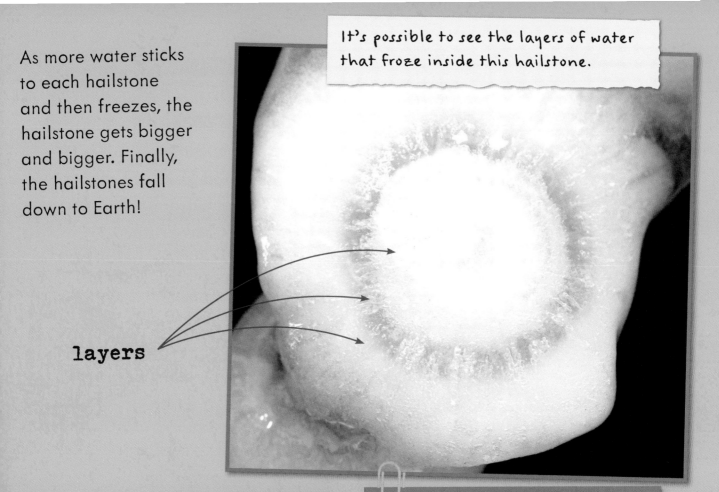

layers

Giant Hailstones

Hailstones are usually about the size of a pea. Sometimes, however, they can be the size of a marble or even a golf ball! In 2010, a hailstone that measured 8 inches (20.3 cm) fell from the sky in Vivian, South Dakota!

the hailstone from Vivian, South Dakota

GIANT ICE PEBBLES

Water can be a liquid, a gas, and a solid. When water gets warm, it becomes vapor. When it freezes, it becomes solid ice. But both water vapor and ice can change to become liquid water again. It's because water can change in this way that we have rain, hailstones, and snow. Now, turn some water into solid ice pebbles with this fun craft activity!

You will need:
- Foil dishes 6 to 8 inches (15 to 20 cm) across
- Water
- Food coloring in different colors
- A paintbrush
- Pretty pebbles, leaves, or flowers
- A thermometer
- Freezing cold weather or a freezer

GET CRAFTING:

1 If it is winter you can make this project outdoors. Put a thermometer outside and after two hours check to see if the red line is on or below 32°F (0°C) on the scale. If it is, it means the weather is cold enough to turn water into ice.

2 If you want to make this craft and the weather is not freezing cold, you can use a freezer.

3 Fill the foil dishes with water.

4 Now comes the really fun part. To make a colored ice pebble, put 5 drops of food coloring into the dish. Stir the water with a paintbrush.

5 You can make clear pebbles, too. Try dropping some real pebbles, leaves, or flowers into the water to add some decoration.

pretty pebbles

colorful leaves

flowers

dishes of water
with food
coloring

6 Leave your ice pebbles to freeze outside. If you are making them in a freezer, put them in the freezer overnight.

7 When the water in the dishes has frozen solid, tip the pebbles out of the dishes. Now they are ready to be placed in your backyard or schoolyard.

8 In winter, the pebbles will last for as long as the temperature stays low. At other times of the year, watch to see how quickly the icy pebbles become water again.

THUNDERSTORMS

With deep rumbles and claps of thunder and bright flashes of lightning, a thunderstorm is one of the most dramatic types of weather.

As a huge, dark thunderstorm cloud moves through the sky, it rubs against the air around it. This makes a type of electricity, called **static electricity**, build up in the cloud.

The electricity produces the flashes of lightning that we see. Lightning flashes travel at 60,000 miles per second (97,000 km/s).

A lightning flash opens up a long hole, or tunnel, in the air. When the flash has passed, the air instantly collapses back into the tunnel. This movement of air causes the rumbling, or cracking, thunder noise.

thunderstorm cloud

lightning

Tornadoes

Sometimes the air inside a thunderstorm cloud begins to spin faster and faster, forming a huge column. When the spinning column hits the ground, it is called a tornado. As it moves along the ground, a tornado can uproot trees and destroy buildings!

tornado damage

27

DAILY WEATHER CHART

This wheel-shaped weather chart can be designed with all the types of weather you see in your area. Then each day, turn the arrow to show that day's weather on your chart.

You will need:

- A paper plate
- A pencil
- A ruler
- A black marker
- Glue
- To make our weather wheel we used paints, bubble wrap, foil, salt, and black paper

- A small piece of colorful cardboard
- A brass fastener
- An adult to be your teammate and to help with cutting

GET CRAFTING:

1 Make a list of the types of weather you have where you live. Choose six types of weather that happen most often.

2 Using the pencil and ruler, draw lines to divide the plate into six equal sections. Then ink in the lines with the marker.

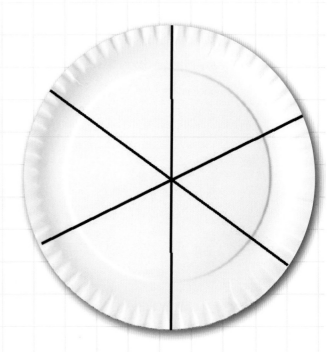

3 Now draw, paint, or glue craft materials to the plate to show the six types of weather you see most. Ask an adult to help you with any cutting. Here's what we did:

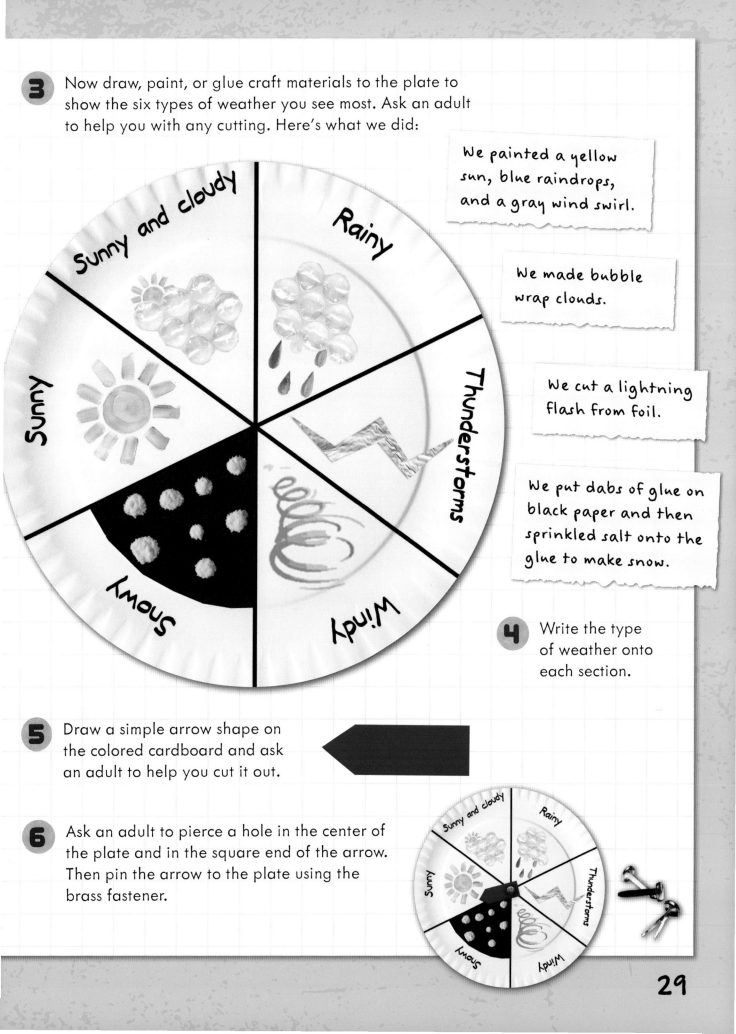

We painted a yellow sun, blue raindrops, and a gray wind swirl.

We made bubble wrap clouds.

We cut a lightning flash from foil.

We put dabs of glue on black paper and then sprinkled salt onto the glue to make snow.

4 Write the type of weather onto each section.

5 Draw a simple arrow shape on the colored cardboard and ask an adult to help you cut it out.

6 Ask an adult to pierce a hole in the center of the plate and in the square end of the arrow. Then pin the arrow to the plate using the brass fastener.

GLOSSARY

blizzard (BLIH-zurd)
A storm during which lots of snow falls and there are very strong winds.

crops (KRAHPS)
Plants that are grown in large quantities on a farm.

degree (dih-GREE)
A unit of measurement used to measure how hot or cold something is.

drought (DROWT)
A time when no rain, or less rain than usual, falls in an area.

gas (GAS)
Matter, such as water vapor, that is neither a solid nor a liquid.

liquid (LIH-kwed)
Something that flows, such as water, and changes its shape to fit any container it is placed in.

static electricity
(STA-tik ih-lek-TRIH-suh-tee)
A type of electricity that is produced when two things are rubbed together.

symbol (SIM-bul)
A picture that is used to stand for something else.

water cycle (WAH-ter SY-kul)
The process in which water moves from Earth up into the sky to make clouds, and back down to Earth again.

water vapor (WAH-ter VAY-pur)
Water that has turned into a gas.

Websites

https://climatekids.nasa.gov/menu/weather-and-climate/

https://www.weatherwizkids.com/

https://www.ducksters.com/science/weather.php

Publisher's note to parents and teachers: Our editors have reviewed the websites listed here to make sure they're suitable for students. However, websites may change frequently. Please note that students should always be supervised when they access the internet.

READ MORE

Bradley, Doug. *20 Things You Didn't Know About Weather (Did You Know? Earth Science)*. New York: Rosen Publishing, 2023.

Francis, Alex. *What's the Weather? An Alien's Guide (Early Bird Nonfiction Readers)*. Minneapolis, MN: Lerner Publishing Group, 2021.

London, Martha. *Thunderstorms (Extreme Weather)*. Minneapolis, MN: Abdo Publishing, 2020.

INDEX